In-Line Skating

by Gail Blasser Riley

COVER-TO-COVER BOOKS

Book Design: Mark Hagenberg
Photo Research: Lisa Lorimor

Dedication

To James—the best son in the world—whose intellect, input, wit, and encouragement made this book possible

Special Thanks

Thanks to the Ankeny, Iowa, Parks and Recreation Department for the use of the skate park

Image Credits:
© Associated Press: pp. 7, 42; © Al Fuchs/NewSport/Corbis: p. 46; © Duomo/CORBIS: p. 44;
© Jill Kelley, Digital Images, L.L.C.: back cover, pp. 3, 5, 12, 15, 16 (bottom), 17, 18, 19, 21, 23 (top), 25, 26 (bottom), 31, 33, 34, 35, 36, 37, 38, 50 (bottom left, bottom center), 51, 57, 59;
© Larry Kasperek/NewSport/Corbis: p. 41; © National Museum of Rollerskating, Lincoln, Nebraska: pp. 8, 10, 11; © Nicolas Sautiez/ACM/Corbis: p. 47;
© Tom Kimmell Photography/USA Hockey Inline: p. 62; USA Hockey Inline: p. 61;
© Scott Walker/Big Day Importing: p. 22

Clipart.com: pp. 13, 14, 16 (top), 20, 23 (bottom), 28, 39, 48, 49, 53, 55, 56;
Photos.com: cover, pp. 9, 24, 26 (center), 27, 29, 30, 32, 52, 54, 60

Perfection Learning® Corporation
1000 North Second Avenue, P.O. Box 500, Logan, Iowa 51546-0500.
Tel: 1-800-831-4190 • Fax: 1-800-543-2745
perfectionlearning.com

1   2   3   4   5   6   PP   09   08   07   06   05   04

Paperback ISBN 0-7891-6315-2
Cover Craft® ISBN 0-7569-2964-4

Contents

History

of In-Line Skating

1760 In Belgium, musician Joseph Merlin invents a skate with one row of wheels.

1819 In France, M. Petibledin **patents** the first roller skate. It has one row of wheels.

1863 American James Plimpton makes the roller skate more useful. Each skate has two rows of wheels that use a rubber cushion to attach the wheel axles. The design allows skaters to make curving turns.

1884 Pin ball bearing wheels make skate movement easier and skates lighter.

1901 Roller hockey teams begin playing throughout Europe.

1902 The first public skating rink is opened in Chicago.

1936 The first world championships in roller hockey are held in Germany.

1937 The first World Speed Championships are held in Italy.

1966 The first in-line boot skate is made in Chicago.

1979 Ice hockey players Scott and Brennan Olson create a modern in-line skate.

1983 Scott Olson forms a company called Rollerblade, Inc.

1991 The first in-line-skating magazine is published.

1992 In-line skating competitions begin.

Roller hockey is played as a demonstration sport at the 1992 Summer Olympic Games in Spain.

1995 The Aggressive Skaters Association (ASA) is formed.

The first X Games (Extreme Games) are held.

1999 In-line skating gets its own U.S. postage stamp.

Demonstration Sports

It takes many years for a sport to become part of the Olympics. Once a sport has met the requirements and been approved, it appears as a demonstration sport at the Games. Athletes compete in the sport, but they don't receive medals. A sport may make several appearances as a demonstration sport before it finally becomes a regular Olympic event.

Chapter 1

Catching Air!

The crowd looks skyward as the skater takes his spot at the top of the **vert ramp**. He's coming into the 2001 X Games hoping to be one of the top three skaters. The skater has taken home a medal the past two years. Will he medal again at the X Games today?

The skater drops onto the vert ramp and smoothly skates up the other side, **catching air** at the top. He catches more air on the other side. On the way back, he **rockets** air, kicking out his feet and reaching toward his skates.

He tries for a **switch 900**. He makes two-and-a-half turns in the air. The crowd cheers. He rolls back up to a flip. He soars back above the ramp while spinning in a **flat spin 720**.

Now the skater sets up with a **grind** for his next trick. He's well into his **run**. Will he go for it? Will he try his biggest trick? The crowd watches. All gazes are fixed on the skater. The crowd can't wait. He goes for it! Way above the ramp, he spins like a top, three full rotations! He's at least 20 feet in the air!

The skater lands. Even without too much speed, he sets up for a **fakie 900**. It is amazing that he still airs above the **coping**. Moving backward, sailing through the air, he spins two-and-a-half rotations, landing backward. A roar rises from the crowd.

Eito Yasutoko and his younger brother, Takeshi, are two of the strongest in-line skaters in the world.

The competition is over. How has he scored? The skater has medalled again!

Extreme Sports: Aggressive In-Line Skating

What is an extreme sport? The word *extreme,* when used to describe a sport, means "involving a high degree of physical risk." Aggressive in-line skating easily fits the definition.

How does aggressive in-line skating differ from other types of in-line skating? It is not just for recreation. It focuses on tricks.

You'll read more about the tricks in upcoming chapters. But first, read on to learn about the history of the sport, where people in-line skate, and the equipment and gear used.

Chapter 2

Roots in the Past

You've read about an amazing aggressive in-line-skating run. The background for this run began hundreds of years ago. Who created the first skate? Who put just one row of wheels on skates? Where did this sport begin?

The Earliest Skates

America hadn't declared its independence when the first skates rolled through a village in Holland in the early 1700s. The inventor missed ice-skating in the summer. So he nailed wooden spools to strips of wood. Then he hooked the strips of wood to his shoes. Good idea, but the skates didn't work very well.

Merlin's Magic

Many people think that the in-line skate is a new invention. This type of skate has only one row of wheels on each boot, but here's the surprise. Some of the very first skates had only one row of wheels.

Joseph Merlin was a musician from Belgium. In 1760, he thought of an idea for a new type of skate. He made his skates with small metal wheels placed in a single row.

Merlin wanted to introduce his invention to the public in a big way. So he skated right into a party while playing his violin. Fortunately, Merlin had invented something very interesting. Unfortunately, he couldn't control it. He couldn't stop or even steer. As a result, he crashed into a huge mirror. The mirror and Merlin's violin smashed into tiny pieces.

Merlin was ahead of his time with his in-line skates. It would be many years before skates would be developed further.

Petibledin skate

As Smooth as Ice?

The first patent for roller skates was issued in 1819. Monsieur Petibledin of France created a skate by using a wooden sole. Two to four rollers were arranged in a straight line on the bottom of the sole. The rollers were made of several different materials. These included ivory, wood, or copper.

Petibledin said that people using his skates could perform the same tricks they saw ice-skaters perform. Was the claim true? Not exactly. People couldn't turn and curve in these skates. As with earlier skates, the rollers only went straight.

Plimpton's Quad Skates

By 1863, a familiar sight was rolling along in America. James Plimpton invented an entirely new kind of skate. Plimpton decided to use two sets of wheels. Because *quad* means "four," Plimpton's skate is often called the *quad skate*.

Plimpton quad skate

James Plimpton

Plimpton placed one set of wheels under the ball of the foot. The other set supported the heel. Plimpton made the wheels from boxwood. They worked on rubber cushions. The cushions allowed the axles to move so the skater could control the wheels.

Finally, someone had invented a dry-land skate that could move in a curve. The public was delighted. Plimpton had created a skate that would allow people to turn, curve, and even skate backward!

People were wild about the quad skate. In-line skates began to disappear.

The Hockey Players' Goal

The in-line skate made a small return in 1960. A company in Chicago made an in-line skate with a boot. It looked very much like the modern in-line skate. This skate, though, was not comfortable. Plus, it didn't move or stop easily.

Years later in 1979, brothers Scott and Brennan Olson wished they could find a way to train for ice hockey during the few months when ice was not easy to find in Minnesota.

One day, they were looking through boxes in a used-sporting-goods store. The brothers stumbled across an old pair of skates. They looked like the skates from the Chicago company. The brothers changed the wheels to ones made of a **polyurethane** material. This lightweight material was smooth and even, and the wheels moved easily. The Olsons also added a brake. The skates worked just like ice skates, only with wheels on the ground instead of blades on ice.

In-Line Skating Takes Off

The Olsons' in-line skates caused a skating boom all over the world. In-line-skating magazines hit the newsstands. In-line videos flew off store shelves. By 1995, the Aggressive Skaters Association (ASA) welcomed members from all over the world. ASA began to host **amateur** and **professional** in-line-skating competitions. Another company hosted the X Games, a popular and important in-line competition for extreme-sports enthusiasts.

In-line skating had become important in and outside of the sports world. In 1997, a select group of skaters from around the world began a global skating tour. Their goal was to work for unity, or oneness, through sports. South African President Nelson Mandela served as Patron-in-Chief of the project. The skaters earned support and **donations** from world leaders. All the proceeds went to the Nelson Mandela Children's Fund.

The United States Postal Service created stamps in 1999 to honor four different extreme sports. Many envelopes and packages traveled to their destinations with the image of an in-line skater catching air.

Chapter 3

A Place to Skate

Major Kinds of In-Line Skating

Where do skaters skate? Sounds like an easy question, doesn't it? But it's not quite as simple as it sounds. There are many types of in-line skating. Where people usually skate depends on the kind of skating they do.

Not everyone wants to grind, jump, flip, and spin. For them, recreational or fitness skating is the way to go. Recreational skating is getting from one place to another just for the pleasure of skating. Fitness skating is done for exercise, to stay in shape, and to maintain one's health. Skates for these types of skating have toe stops for braking. Aggressive skates do not.

Some in-line skaters enjoy speed skating. Others might play roller hockey. Special equipment is available for each of these in-line sports.

Aggressive In-Line Skating

Let's take a close look at aggressive in-line skating, an extreme sport. *Aggressive* means "having a driving force." There is certainly a driving force behind aggressive skating! This type of skating is characterized by its tricks. There are three basic types of in-line skating—street, park, and vert.

STREET SKATING

Street skaters do their tricks on things they find outside. They use railings and curbs for grinding. They jump across stairs or do stair rides. Even large piles of dirt can be exciting as skaters jump over them. Concrete benches and tables also provide surfaces for in-line street skaters. Concrete walls become surfaces for in-line tricks.

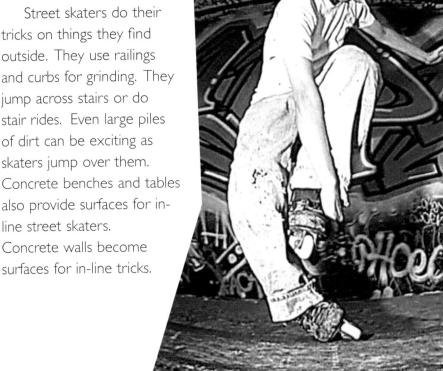

Skaters usually prefer just one kind of in-line skating. Some of the best-known street skaters include Brian Shima, Josh Petty, Mike Johnson, and Dre Powell.

Why do street skaters say they prefer this kind of aggressive in-line skating? They like the freedom of skating outside. Some live in areas where there are many handrails and ledges—perfect for skating. Street skaters often say they like the variety of equipment offered by street skating.

Skate parks have the same types of ramps and other equipment. But on the street, there's almost no end to the places where skaters can do their tricks. Because skate parks may charge a fee for admission, some skaters prefer to save their money and skate "on the streets."

I'll Take the Stairs

A stair ride is a trick where the skater skates down the stairs forward, backward, or sideways.

Cautions for Street Skating

Many business owners and city officials have lobbied to have street skating banned. They point to the property that has been damaged by skaters. Concrete benches, flower containers, and curbs have been worn down and even broken. Railings have come loose and are not safe. Plus businesses must pay higher **liability** insurance in case a skater is injured on their property.

Always check the local laws before taking up street skating.

Park Skating

Everything skaters need is set up and ready to go when they arrive at skate parks—ramps and pipes, grinding rails, and vert walls. Most skate parks are inside buildings. Others are outside in parklike settings.

Park skaters say they like this type of skating because they can skate as soon as they arrive. They don't have to worry about finding ramps and rails of their own. They don't have to worry about bans against skating.

Many park skaters enjoy seeing the same friends when they skate. Often, they support one another and know which types of trick each is trying to perfect.

Indoor skate parks have an advantage. Rain or shine, skaters can take to the rails and ramps! Some of the best-known park skaters include Jaren Grob and Sven Boekhorst.

LAUNCH RAMP

Skaters usually use these ramps to launch themselves into the air for spins.

LAUNCH BOX

Launch boxes often have rails and metal edges. The boxes come in many heights. Skaters can skate across the boxes. They can use the metal edges and rails for grinding.

SPINE

Skaters skate up and over, then down the spine, often doing tricks as they go. The coping is the metal at the top. It is used for grinds and other tricks. The spine can be made by putting two quarter pipes together.

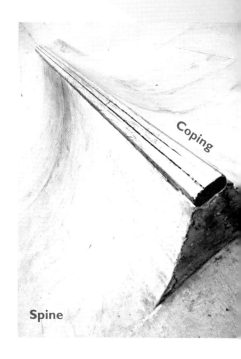

Spine

PYRAMID

Pyramids can be found in all shapes and sizes at skate parks. Skaters do all sorts of tricks on this type of equipment.

QUARTER PIPE, HALF PIPE, VERT

This equipment allows skaters to gain speed to do tricks. Skaters can **drop in** from the high level at the top of a vert wall.

Skater landing on a quarter pipe

KINK

This is the slanted part of coping used to go to a lower level of a quarter pipe.

SPEED HUMP

Skaters can roll over a speed hump to get more speed. They can launch over the top of the speed hump to move faster.

GRIND BOX

The metal edges on the grind box are perfect for grinding.

FLAT BANK

Skaters skate down this ramp to get more speed. This diagonal ramp is a flat piece of metal or wood. It is not curved like a quarter pipe. Some large flat banks have a small curve in the last half foot.

LEDGE

Skaters grind on a ledge. At skate parks, a ledge is usually made of wood covered in angle iron. This is a piece of metal shaped like a triangle without a third side. It is nailed into the wood. Other ledges at skate parks have coping nailed into them.

Ledge

Handrail and pyramid

Stair rail

GRIND RAIL

There are many different types of rails. The usual type of grind rail is portable. It can be moved from one part of the park to another. Grind rails are usually about one foot high.

HANDRAIL

Handrails are not usually found in a skate park. These are slanted rails at the sides of stairs. Some skate parks will try to imitate a handrail by putting a rail on the flat bank of a box.

VERT SKATING

    Strong tricks are important in vert skating. The tricks high above the crowd are rated by judges. Vert skaters love the thrill of launching themselves into the air to perform.

    For vert competition, a skater must drop into a half pipe. Then the skater launches high into the air. Skaters often do big spins high above the coping. Usually, the higher the spin, the more the judges are impressed. Vert skaters also do grinds on the half pipe. Most of the pros prefer to do switchups, moving from one trick to another without a break.

    You may have seen vert skating competitions on TV. Vert competitions are usually international, so it's not unusual to see skaters from all over the world competing.

Chapter 4

The Essentials

First Things First

It's no surprise that in-line skaters must think about the skates first. It's important to buy aggressive in-line skates. These skates have no toe stops or brakes. In-line skaters use certain moves to stop themselves. Aggressive skates allow skaters to do grinds. Recreational skates do not.

In-line skates have many interchangeable parts. This is important because parts of the skate can wear out quickly due to aggressive skating moves. Skating on rough pavement can damage some, but not all, parts of the skates.

Some skaters find the wheels of one skate work best for them. But they might like the cuff or boot of another skate. So they "build" their own pair of skates.

Boot

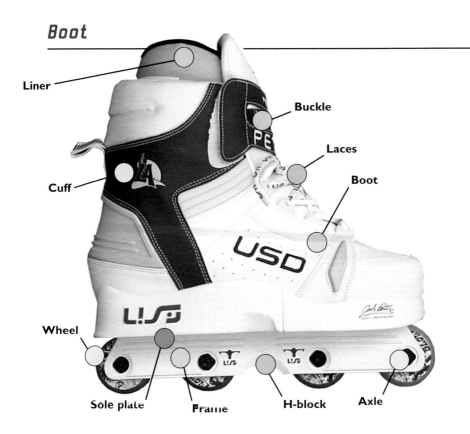

Liner

Cuff

Buckle

Laces

Boot

Wheel

Sole plate

Frame

H-block

Axle

LINER

The liner is a piece inside the boot. It is exactly the same shape as the boot. The purpose of the liner is to make the skater's foot secure and comfortable. In-line skaters do not skate without a liner. Some skates have soft shells, or outer parts, so a good liner becomes even more important.

Skaters make liner choices based on a number of factors. The skater wants the liner to give strong support. When a move exerts pressure on the ankle, the skater needs a very supportive liner to keep the ankle secure.

Skaters also think about comfort when choosing a liner. Most soft liners feel more comfortable, but they may not be as secure as a harder liner. Think about buying a pair of shoes.

One person might find a pair of shoes very comfortable. Another person might find the same pair uncomfortable. It's the same with skate liners.

CUFF

Cuffs support the ankles. Aside from the liner, the cuff is the highest section of the skate. Some skaters like to change cuffs to add additional support or style. The cuff is usually the easiest and least expensive part of the skate to change.

BUCKLE

Some skates come with buckles. Others come with laces. Still others have both. All provide some support for the ankles. Laces can allow for a tighter skate than buckles. But buckles are easier to adjust while skating. Skates with buckles are quicker to put on and take off.

Frame

The frame holds the wheels and the boot together. The H-block attaches to the frame between the second and third wheels. It allows skaters to do tricks such as frontside, backside, unity, fast slide, and others.

The Universal Frame System (UFS) makes it easier to attach different parts from different manufacturers to a frame. Before the UFS, skaters could only use frames that would fit on boots from the same manufacturer. Boots were drilled with holes in different places. Frames were made with different kinds of connectors.

Today, more and more frame companies are changing the connections of their frames to UFS. Most companies now make boots that work with these frames. Skaters can now choose the frames they want for their skates.

Skaters choose frames for many reasons. They consider the material used to make the frame, how long the frame will last, the color of the frame, and the frame's H-block.

Sole Plate

The sole plate is a long strip of hard plastic or other hard material. It is often made with a nonstick substance that makes the plate glide smoothly when doing grinds.

The sole plate is attached to the bottom of the frame. Using the sole plate, the skater can do a variety of tricks. The inside of the plate is the negative plate. The outside plate is the positive, or sole, plate. The negative plate is smaller and is not used for tricks as much as the positive plate.

Many skaters prefer a wide sole plate. This makes it easier to perform a grind without slipping.

Axles

Axles are attached through holes in the frame. The wheels are attached to the axle.

Wheels

The correct wheels are important. Experienced skaters often change the wheels that come on their skates. They learn exactly which wheels they like best.

SIZE

Shorter wheels make moves easier and more stable. But they also make movement slower. Of course, this means that taller wheels give greater speed, but aren't as easy on the moves. Most aggressive skaters use the shorter wheels. The shorter wheels help them grind better and have better control of their tricks.

ANTI-ROCKERS

Anti-rockers are smaller than average skating wheels. They are put in the second and third slots of the frame next to the H-block. Anti-rockers give the skater more space near the H-block. Anti-rockers are made of a material that's used for the core of most wheels. This material is slicker and smoother. Anti-rockers make grinds easier because the smaller wheels are smoother. Also, they don't get in the way and slow the skater down.

BEARINGS

Each wheel has two bearings inside. These make the wheels turn smoothly. It is important to keep the bearings clean and well-oiled. Skaters often take out their wheels and wash them with special bearing **lubricant** or wet paper towels. They are careful to dry the bearings after cleaning. Advanced skaters are familiar with the ABEC (Annual Bearing Engineering Council) ratings for bearings. They think about the rating when choosing bearings.

Helmet

Elbow pads

Knee pads

Wrist guards

Helmet

It's important that skaters always wear helmets. Helmets are required equipment at most skate parks. The helmet should not be loose. It should remain buckled while the skater is skating. It's a good idea to ask whether the helmet you are thinking of buying is approved by SNELL, ASTM, ANSI, or another group known for safety. This should ensure that the helmet is strong enough to do its job. It's important for aggressive in-line skaters to be certain they are purchasing a helmet that is designed for aggressive skating.

Many skaters like to put stickers on their helmets. These stickers often come from in-line skate parks and companies that make in-line skate products. A skater's helmet can be a road map of the skater's experiences. It can show where the skater has skated and whose products the skater likes.

Knee Pads

Falls and crashes are unavoidable when learning to skate as well as when learning new tricks. Snug-fitting knee pads cushion a fall. They protect the skin and also protect the area under the knee from injury. A serious knee injury can end a skater's career. It can even make walking difficult or impossible.

Wrist Guards and Elbow Pads

Which part of the body is most often injured while in-line skating? It's the wrist! Skaters often use their hands to break their falls. This is a natural **reflex**. Wrist guards provide protection and absorb the shock of pounding against the floor or pavement.

Wrist guards also cover the hands to prevent skid burns and cuts.

Elbow pads can help protect a skater in a sideways fall.

Shin Guards

You may not see shin guards as often as you see other skating gear. Some skaters wear guards to protect their shins all the time. Others choose to wear shin guards only after a shin injury.

Shins are often hurt when one of the skates doesn't lock onto the grind surface. The shin can smack hard against the grinding surface. Shin guards offer protection against pain and possible injury.

Skating Backpack

Skaters sometimes like to carry their skates with them. Skating backpacks are made with space for the skates and safety gear.

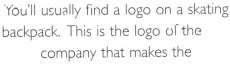

Straps on a skating backpack usually buckle together to keep the skates securely in place. Many skating backpacks have holders for CD players.

You'll usually find a logo on a skating backpack. This is the logo of the company that makes the backpack. It might also be the logo of a company that makes skates.

Chapter 5

Love Those Moves!

What are the tricks used in extreme in-line skating? Grinds, grabs, spins, flips, and inverts are some of the most common. Dozens of variations have been created for each move. And don't forget the most important move of all—stopping!

Stop!

Before you learn about tricks, take a look at one of the basics—a stop. You've read that aggressive in-line skates do not have brakes. How do these skaters stop? They skate into a T-**stance**. This means that the back skate is dragged behind the front foot. The back skate forms the top line of a capital T and the front foot forms the line coming down from it.

Some advanced skaters stop by quickly jumping sideways to break their momentum. This is called a *hockey stop* and is used by ice and roller hockey players to stop or change direction suddenly This move can be difficult. It's easy to slip into a slide from this move.

Soul Grinds

In soul grinds, skaters hook up, or place, the sole plate of the back skate onto a rail or ledge. The H-block of the front skate is hooked up and turned inward. This grind is thought of as the most basic. It is the building block of grinds that require the sole plate. When skaters talk about soul grinds, they talk about the soul foot. This is the foot that has the sole plate hooked up to the ledge.

To do a soul grind, the skater skates alongside a railing and jumps onto it. The skater connects the soul foot and the H-block on the rail. It's important to keep the knees bent for balance. The trick is complete after the skater slides across the rail and jumps off.

VARIATIONS ON SOUL GRINDS

Acid leaving the soul foot on the grind surface, pointing forward, while angling the front foot in the opposite direction

Acid Miszou grinding on the boot with one foot while placing the other foot on the sole plate. The grinding foot is behind you and bent inward. This is one of the most popular moves.

Alley-Oop Soul sliding backward for the soul grind

Topside Soul doing a soul grind while going topside and backward

Which Side?

Topside, farside, and backside all refer to how the skater approaches and faces the bar or curb while performing the move.

Biscuit bending the knees while doing a soul grind so that the toes of both feet point inward

Fishbrain grinding topside with one skate while pulling up the other skate

Kind Grind doing a topside alley-oop miszou

Makio grinding on one foot with the sole plate. This is one of the most basic grinds. It is often done while grabbing the foot that is not grinding.

Makio

Mistrial doing a miszou with the back skate bent inward and toes turning out

Miszou grinding with the front skate in soul position and the back skate perpendicular behind it

Negative Grind doing any kind of grind using the sole plate, using the inside—negative sole plate—instead of the positive plate. For example, doing a miszou with the inside plate instead of the outside plate would be a negative miszou.

Stub Soul doing a makio with both feet, but with one foot on its negative plate and one foot on its positive plate

Sweatstance doing a topside miszou

Topside Soul doing a soul grind while bending the ankle of the soul foot so the frame goes on the ledge at the top of a ramp

Truespin doing a spin, usually a 270, over the coping before a grind

Frontside royale

Frontside and Backside Grinds

For a frontside grind, the skater hooks up H-blocks on both skates to the rail while facing the rail. For a backside grind, the skater hooks up H-blocks on both skates with the back to the rail. A frontside grind is thought of as a basic grind. It leads to making other grinds easier. The frontside grind is usually the first grind a skater learns on a half pipe.

VARIATIONS ON FRONTSIDE AND BACKSIDE GRINDS

Backslide doing a royale while picking up the front foot

Backside royale

Cab Driver doing a Texan while wheels on each skate touch each other

Fast slide doing a frontside while picking up the back foot

Royale doing a frontside or backside grind while bending the ankles in the opposite direction of the slide

Tabernacle doing a frontside while turning one foot 180°

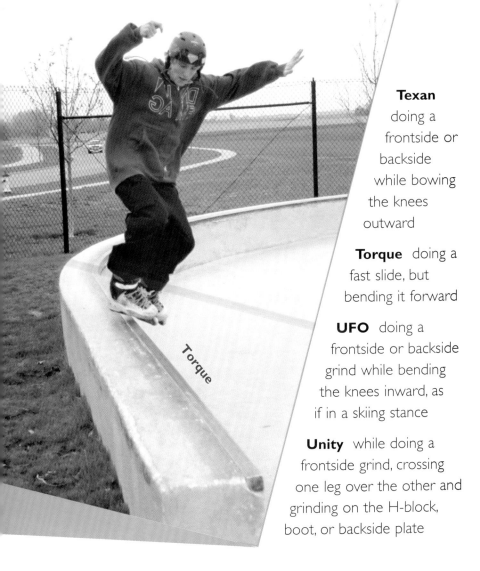

Torque

Texan doing a frontside or backside while bowing the knees outward

Torque doing a fast slide, but bending it forward

UFO doing a frontside or backside grind while bending the knees inward, as if in a skiing stance

Unity while doing a frontside grind, crossing one leg over the other and grinding on the H-block, boot, or backside plate

Grabs

When a skater jumps into the air and grabs one or both skates, the move is called a *grab*. This is a move done for style.

TYPES OF GRABS

Liu Kang kicking one foot out while bending the other foot under the thigh and grabbing the skate of the bent foot at the frame or boot. The skater appears to be in almost a sitting position during this grab.

Method bending backward while kicking both heels up, pulling on the ankles

Mute bending the knees and grabbing the boot of the right skate with the left hand or the left skate with the right hand

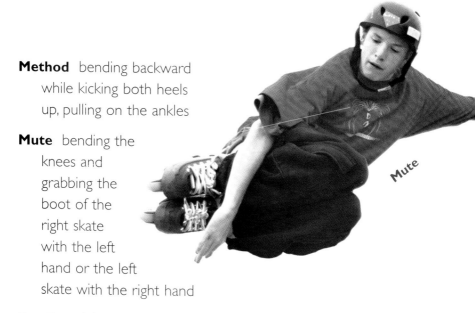

Mute

Parallel doing a mute while grabbing the outside sole plate instead of the boot

Rocket sticking both feet straight out in front of you while touching your toes

Safety Grab bending the knees and grabbing the sole plate or frame of the right skate with the right hand or the left skate with the left hand. Knees can be pulled up or to the side.

Liu Kang

Spins

Spins are named by the number of degrees in the revolutions. For example, half of a spin is a 180. A full single spin is a 360. A spin-and-a-half trick is called a 540.

Spins are also named for the position of the body during the spin. For example, in a flat spin, the skater gets air, turns the body to a horizontal position, spins, and then lands upright. A skater can do a 180 flat spin, a 360 flat spin, or a 540 flat spin. You get the picture. In a bio spin, the skater is upside down during the spin. As with the flat spin, the skater can do a 180, a 360, a 540, or something larger.

180 over a spine

TYPES OF SPINS

96 doing a royale without touching the boot

180 Half spin or revolution. Face a wall. Jump up and spin around and land with back to the wall.

360 A full spin. Face a wall. Jump up and spin around and land facing the wall again.

540 One and a half spins before landing

720 Two full spins before landing

900 Two and a half spins before landing

1080 Three full spins before landing

Skaters work continually to improve their spins and increase the number of revolutions they can complete.

Inverts and Wall Rides

An invert is like a handstand on coping. In an invert, the skater skates up a vert ramp and grabs the coping with one hand, pushing up into the position of a handstand. Sometimes, the skater flips all the way over the coping and lands on the opposite side.

To do a wall ride, the skater speeds along on a flat surface and jumps up to a wall. The skater then rides sideways across the wall.

Invert

Chapter 6

They Know Their Stuff!

Many great in-line skaters have dropped in and skated their way into history. You can read about a few of the pros here. Each of these skaters has won dozens of competitions.

What makes an in-line skater a pro? A pro, short for professional, is a skater who makes money from skating. To be qualified as a pro and allowed to skate in professional ASA competitions, a skater must place in the top five of the amateur division of the world championships. Street skaters reach pro status by being paid for their skating by a skating sponsor, such as a skate company.

In-line skating pros are some of the best skaters you will see anytime, anywhere. They have had a great deal of experience and are among the strongest skaters in the world. Their skill level is startling!

Eito and Takeshi Yasutoko

Eito Yasutoko, nicknamed Eight, was born in Osaka, Japan, on July 29, 1983. His high-flying moves are inherited. His parents, Yuki and Tomoko Yasutoko, are former roller disco dancers. They own and run a skate park in Japan.

Eito and his younger brother, Takeshi, have skated since they were two years old. Both boys became professionals in 1995. Because of the skating background in the Yasutoko family, they are known as the "first skate family of Japan."

Takeshi, whose nickname is Samurai, was the youngest person ever to go pro. He was only 9. At 11, he was the youngest athlete to compete at the X Games. Four years later, Takeshi became the youngest vert skater to ever win a medal at the X Games.

Eito and Takeshi are two of the finest skaters ever to take to a vert ramp. Eito claimed the gold medal and Takeshi took the silver in the vert competition in San Francisco in 2000. They both landed 1080s. This was the first time 1080s had been landed by two skaters in the same competition. In the 2002 X Games, Takeshi took the gold medal, and Eito received the silver. In the 2003 X Games, the brothers reversed places with Eito winning the gold and Takeshi taking the silver. Without a doubt, the brothers will be a **dominant** force in this sport for years to come.

Jaren Grob in the 2002 X Games

Jaren Grob

How do skaters know Jaren Grob? He's the "Monster." He earned this title because of his huge style. He's also known as "Air Grob."

Jaren was born in Utah. He was a young boy when he got his first pair of skates at a local discount store. Wheels became a huge part of his life right away. Before long, he started skating at a nearby skate park. Unfortunately, it burned down. But that didn't keep Jaren off of his wheels.

Jaren put a skate ramp in his backyard. It was 11 feet tall! By 1996, Jaren was performing skating demos at schools. He just had to be on his skates as much as possible. Where did Jaren go next? The answer might surprise you. He performed in the circus! Then he returned to his home state of Utah.

By 1999, Jaren had revved up his competition. He ranked third in street skating on the ASA Pro Tour. He also won the Rookie of the Year award. Grob is a top-ranked skater. He has competed in vert and street, taking home many wins and a great deal of prize money.

Fans say that Jaren hasn't started to feel as though he's "too good" for others. Even though he's ranked right up there at the top, he continues to put a great deal of work into his skating. Jaren summed up his feelings about skating in a recent newspaper interview. "Even if I couldn't make a dime from skating, I'd still be doing it."

Cesar Mora

Cesar Mora is admired for his remarkable skating ability. Cesar first trained in another sport—soccer. He was a serious soccer player from the time he was 5. By the time he was 19, he had joined the Australian National Team. He traveled throughout the world to compete. His devotion to soccer formed a strong foundation for his skating.

How did Mora begin in-line skating? His car wouldn't run. He needed a way to get around in the city. He watched someone skating through town, and the idea of skating to get to where he was going stuck with him.

Later, Cesar took a job at a skate shop. One of the customers invited him to skate. At first, skates hurt Cesar's feet, but he kept skating. He practiced hard. Before he knew it, he was on the way to the X Games.

Cesar Mora in the 1999 Summer X Games

By 1999, Cesar had become the only skater to land a 1080 in competition. About his skating, he said, "I would like to give kids who are ten years old today the same rewarding experience I've had with skating."

Cesar was first recognized for his huge airs and large numbers of spins. By 2002, he had become the only skater to compete in every vert final competition in the X Games. He became a legend for his disasters, his 900, and his fakie 900.

Cesar has goals and hopes for skaters. He says that he wants to "teach why drugs are no good and why school's important . . . there's so much more about skating. We're people before we're skaters, and we're people after we're skaters."

What's a Disaster?

This skating move was perfected by Cesar Mora. The skater catches air just before entering the ramp, lands on the coping, and spins into the ramp.

Brian Shima

Skaters know that Brian Shima's claim to fame lies in doing things his own way. This skater is known all over the world! He is very creative. He likes to try all sorts of new tricks. People say that he skates "huge" and is among the very best of the best. What did Brian say when asked what he likes best about skating? He likes the feeling of freedom. Brian says that, in skating, you can do whatever you want and have fun with it.

What are a few of the tricks Brian uses to wow a crowd? How about a topside soul, disaster alley-oop, a 180, a backside royale, abstract 540, and a soul grind to 540? Now that's huge!

Other skaters enjoy talking about how much they admire Shima. They are very impressed by Brian's unusual style. Skater Pat Lennen says, "He's got a really different style . . . He can take a basic trick and make it look so smooth and stylish that people just really appreciate our sport."

Brian is such a strong skater that a type of skate now bears his name. He is best known as a street skater.

Fabiola da Silva

Fabiola da Silva is Fabby to her friends. She's also sometimes called Fab—for Fabiola and for "fabulous." Fabby is one of the best in-line skaters in the world. She was born in Brazil in 1979. Her full name is Fabiola Oliveira Samoes da Silva.

Fabiola's mom was athletic when she was young. She knew that Fabby loved to skate, so she saved her money for two years to buy skates for Fabby. The price of skates in Brazil was much higher than in the United States.

Chris Edwards, one of the very first in-line skaters, traveled to Brazil for a skating exhibition. He saw Fabby skate. He was so impressed that he invited her to come to the United States. She skated in the 1996 X Games when she was only 15.

Fabiola da Silva in the 2003 Gravity Games

Fabiola now lives in
the United States. For many years,
there have been separate competitions for
men and women. Fabby wanted to prove that a young
woman could place in the top ten in a men's competition.

Because of Fabby, the ASA **adopted** the "Fabiola Rule."
The rule states that women can compete in the men's vert final.
Fabiola has placed in the top 10 in men's competitions several
times. She has even taken third!

When Fabiola was young, professional skaters like Cesar
Mora and Chris Edwards were her role models. She has now
become a role model for others. Fabiola works to encourage
young women to compete in aggressive skating. It is said that she
is never too busy to say "hello" to a fan or to sign an autograph.

Fabiola shows that an athlete can be at the top of a sport
and still be a *good* sport. After being beaten at the Gravity
Games by Martina Svobodova, Fabby was asked how she felt
about coming in second. She said, "That's cool. When you
compete, you have to be prepared to win or lose. And I'm
happy because this was a chance for somebody new. Martina
deserved it; she did a great run."

Fabiola is such a good skater that she was asked to play the **stunt double** for an actress in a movie. She did all the skating tricks. Maybe you've seen *Brink!* Perhaps you thought you were watching the actress do her own skating tricks. But you were really watching Fabby!

How does Fabiola feel about being at the top of her game? She said, "I hate it when guys say girls can't do things. That is so out of my head now. Actually, that is what pushes me to be better. I just want to show that girls can do anything they want to."

Other Pros

Aaron Feinberg is a street skater. He tries everything, and there are very few skaters who have his strength and creativity in skating. Feinberg became a pro in 1997 and quickly earned more wins than any other street skater ever had. He topped the X Games by the age of 16.

Taig Khris began skating vert as a pro in 1996. He was the first skater to nail a double back flip in competition. Skating isn't the only time Khris shows his creative talent. He is also a fine piano player!

Taig Khris practicing on a half-pipe

Chapter 7

There's More!

Aggressive in-line skaters love their sport. But aggressive is not the only kind of in-line skating. Each type of in-line skating has its own special flavor.

The Need for Speed: Speed Skating

Some skaters have a big need for speed. Jumps, spins, and grinds don't take these skaters where they want to go. They only get that **rush of adrenaline** when going as fast as possible.

Speed skates are very different from aggressive in-line skates. Speed skates have five wheels instead of four. The wheels extend far past the boot.

The boot is also very different. It is lower than the aggressive boot. The lower boot gives the skater more freedom in motion. The skater can lean, stretch, and go greater distances after pushing off each time. Most speed skates have built-in heel brakes.

The speed skater's helmet is more pointed than the aggressive skater's helmet. This design reduces wind resistance.

Some competitions offer cash prizes to winners. But most speed skaters just skate to win. They like the feeling of zipping around a track. Most competitions are held outdoors and racers skate about 6 miles. That's the same distance as running around a football field about 42 times! Of course, there are shorter—and longer—races.

In-liners who speed skate must have strength and endurance—the ability to go long distances. They train hard to prepare for competitions. They learn to pace themselves during races. They know they must save enough energy to get them to the finish line.

Got Game? Playing Team Sports on Skates

Shooting hoops? Scoring goals? These may not be the first ideas that pop into your head as you think about in-line skating. Most types of in-line skating are designed for one skater rather than a team of skaters working together on a playing surface to score points. That's not the case with roller hockey and roller basketball. These games prove that sports can be taken to a new place when skates roll into the picture. Of all these types of in-line skating, roller hockey has been popular for the longest time.

Roller Hockey

As you know, in-line skating has its roots in hockey. So in-line hockey play has been around as long as in-line skating. Skate hockey was even played before the days of in-line skates. It was played on quad skates when it first began.

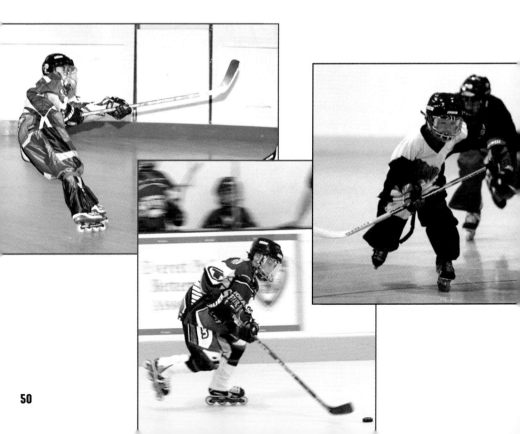

Perhaps you've seen ice hockey games. In-line hockey games are very similar, but an in-line team has one fewer player than the ice hockey team. Each in-line-skating team only has five players, including its goalie.

The skates used for hockey have many of the same features as those used for aggressive in-line skating. The laces are important since they adjust the fit of the skate. The skaters make tight, directed moves, so the boot must fit snugly around the ankle. Hockey skates are made with special types of protection for the feet, since pucks, sticks, and players are flying through the air!

As with all in-line skating, the helmet is a necessary piece of equipment. The helmet for in-line hockey players includes a face guard, of course. And the goalie has even more specialized equipment including extra padding everywhere.

ROLLER BASKETBALL

In-line basketball became popular
during the early 1990s. Today, people of all ages play in-line
basketball. As in other in-line sports, people form competitive
leagues. In-line basketball players usually wear skates with longer
frames than those worn in aggressive skating. In-line basketball
helmets are often the same type used by aggressive skaters.

How is in-line basketball different from basketball games off
wheels? The biggest difference is the size of the team. There are
only four skaters on an in-line team, one fewer than in the
basketball games seen and played off wheels.

In roller basketball, players play with an 18-second shot
clock. After a basket, the opposing team can break out right
away to offense. The players do not have to inbound the ball.
Shots in in-line basketball are worth three or four points, not
two or three points.

And the Beat Goes On: Artistic Skating

Some in-line skaters like to dance on their skates. They follow dance moves for competition or just for fun. Many of their jumps and spins are the same as those done on ice.

At first glance, the artistic in-line skates look like ice skates. They are made with a special toe that helps the skater push off for jumps.

Working Out: Fitness Skating

Getting in shape doesn't have to be boring. Many people choose to in-line skate to get exercise. They usually prepare to skate just as most people prepare for any exercise routine. They stretch and warm their muscles.

Sit-ups? Push-ups? These are exercises you probably know. In-line fitness skaters have exercises created for skating. These exercises are designed to make them stronger and healthier.

Fitness in-liners are usually careful to wear very comfortable clothes and skates. This makes it easier for them to do the exercises on skates. Most fitness in-liners wear skates with longer frames than those of aggressive in-liners. Often the wheels are taller than the wheels on aggressive skates.

Just for Fun: Recreational Skating

How about folks who just want to have fun on skates? They don't want to exercise or dance or jump or spin or play sports. They just want to relax and have fun. The kind of skating they do is called *recreational*.

The skates you usually see in department or discount stores are usually recreational skates. You'll notice that the recreational frame is longer than the aggressive frame. The wheels extend past the skate boot. Recreational in-liners often wear the helmet style that comes to a point in front and in back. Safety gear is still important for recreational skaters. Even though they're not trying tough tricks, they are usually skating outside, and falls are always possible.

Chapter 8

Hints and Tips

Are you planning your first try at in-line skating? Maybe you've been skating for a while. Perhaps you're an expert at in-line skating. No matter what your level is, you'll find tips and hints here that will help you as you skate.

For Beginners

- Don't worry about looking silly. Even the most experienced skaters often fall when they're learning something new.

- Make learning how to stop one of the first things you learn!

- Don't try advanced tricks until you can handle the basics.

- Skate as often as you can. The more practice you get, the better you'll become.

- Check to see if there are any skate parks in your area. You can learn a great deal by watching other skaters.

- Don't let your skates get wet. The bearings can rust. This will make your wheels roll slowly. If your skates do get wet, unscrew your axles, take your wheels out, and use a dry paper towel to soak up all the water on your bearings.

For Street Skaters

- Street skating doesn't mean that you must skate in the street. Sidewalks and other concrete surfaces are fine. Watch for cars backing out of driveways. Be alert to everything going on around you.

- Follow the rules of the road. Obey all traffic laws. If you're a street skater, find out where you are and are not allowed to skate, according to the laws in your area.

- Watch your route carefully. Notice hazards such as cracks, oil, and water on the sidewalk. Even tiny rocks can gum up the works of your wheels.

- Skate on smooth surfaces. A crack running in the direction of your skate wheel can make you lose your balance.

- Remember to stop for people walking in front of you. Be especially careful when young children are nearby.

- Skate only during daylight hours. Drivers and others won't be able to see you at night.

- Feel a fall coming? If you can, lean toward grass or another soft surface. Use your pads and guards to cushion your fall.

For Everyone

- Wear your helmet and other protective gear.

- Thinking about buying skates online instead of going into a store? Here are a few things to keep in mind. You can sometimes get better prices by ordering online, but you won't be able to try on the skates. And many Web sites don't allow returns. Perhaps you'll want to try on skates in a store first. If the price is good, and the people are helpful, you might want to buy your skates in the store. If not, you might think more about ordering online. Don't forget that you'll have to wait for your skates to arrive.

- Talk to other skaters before deciding which skate brand to buy. You can find out more information by researching online. Don't forget to buy aggressive in-line skates if you plan on doing tricks.

- Some skate parks will let you rent skates. Try out several brands.

- Watch for In-line Skating Week in May each year. Local skate parks and many skating organizations have special activities during this week.

- Warm up before trying tricks.

- Check your skates often. Keep them clean and well-oiled. Be sure they are working properly.

- Offer support and help to other skaters.

- Have fun!

Chapter 9

In•Line Skating
Organizations

Want to find out more about in-line skating?
Perhaps you'd like to find out about competitions. What are the
rules? Who makes the rules? How are the rules enforced?
Where do you find the competitions? How do you compete?
Who are the major players? What are their **stats**?

Perhaps you know someone who would like to coach an in-
line skating team. Or maybe you'd like to have more information
about skating gear. Check out in-line skating organizations and
Web sites. You can read about some of them here.

Aggressive Skaters Association (ASA)

Aggressive Skaters Association
13468 Beach Avenue
Marina del Rey, CA 90292
www.ASAskate.com

The ASA holds competitions all over the world for aggressive
in-line skaters. There is a competition for skaters of every
level—amateurs and professionals. The ASA includes a division
for skaters who are 12 years old or younger. These skaters
compete on the amateur circuit. Those who finish at the top of

the amateur circuit have a chance to go pro. Pro skaters can compete in the X Games, the ASA Pro Tour, and the Gravity Games.

You can check out local and regional dates and locations for the events by logging on to the ASA Web site. On the site, you will also find results of past competitions, information about competitions in other countries, and information about pro in-line skaters.

International In-Line Figure Skating Association (IIFSA)

International In-Line Figure Skating Association
201 N. Front St. #306
Wilmington, NC 28401
www.iifsa.com

The International In-Line Figure Skating Association began in 2000. The IIFSA offers tests for in-line figure skaters to pass to win awards. A skater who passes JumpSpin 1 receives a beginner recognition. A skater who passes the JumpSpin 2 becomes a novice and receives a bronze medal. Once a skater reaches the JumpSpin 3 level, the skater advances to the intermediate level and receives a silver medal. The next level is JumpSpin 4, and the skater enters the advanced level and receives a gold medal.

The IIFSA Web site gives more information about how to reach each level. It tells how to become a member and explains the rules for becoming a coach. It offers photos showing in-line figure skaters from across the country.

National In-Line Basketball League (NIBBL) Junior In-Line Basketball League (JIBBL)

135 Rivington St.
Suite 3F
New York, NY 10002

NIBBL describes itself as the "major league of roller basketball." NIBBL was developed by Tom LaGarde. Perhaps his name sounds familiar to you. He is an Olympic gold medalist and NBA player.

NIBBL leagues begin their games in May. League play winds up in October with the championship game. The first games organized by NIBBL were held in 1994. The first interest was in New York, but interest began to grow across the United States.

By 1998, the U. S. National team zipped across the ocean to play in Amsterdam and Portugal. In-line basketball has truly grown in popularity around the world.

In 1999, NIBBL kicked off the NIBBL Globe Rollers. This exhibition team delights folks around the world. It includes ramps in its exhibitions. Think of the Harlem Globetrotters on in-line skates!

JIBBL includes two divisions. They are Jr. JIBBL, for competitors who are 9 to 12 years old, and JIBBL, for competitors who are 13 to 16 years old. The JIBBL program strives to give competitors a feeling of community and teamwork.

National In-Line Racing Association (NIRA)

3234 South Meridan
Wichita, KS 67217
www.sk8nira.com/

The NIRA offers a competitive program for in-line speed skaters. Skaters from across the country follow the same style of in-line speed skating that is used at the world championships. Local clubs can join the NIRA to compete. The NIRA competitions are held on oval tracks, just as the world championships are. This gives skaters a chance to get a feel for the experience of a world championship racer. The track oval has straightaways of equal length. The bends have the same diameter.

International Speed Skating events include relays, Dash for Cash, and Last Out. The relays are for two or three people. Dash for Cash lets each skater skate individually against the clock. At the end of the competition, the skater with the fastest time wins a cash prize. In the Last Out competition, skaters skate around the track as long as they can. The last skater left skating around the track wins the competition.

USA Hockey InLine

1775 Bob Johnson Drive
Colorado Springs, CO 80906-4090
www.usahockey.com/inline/

USA Hockey InLine began in 1994. It is the official in-line hockey program of the national group that governs United States hockey. USA Hockey represents the United States Olympic Committee. It works to help in-line hockey grow and become more popular.

USA Hockey InLine provides playing rules. It also provides guidelines for coaches and competition officials. The group has divisions for boys and girls.

The USA Hockey InLine Web site offers information for players and coaches. For players, the site gives dates and locations of upcoming events. For coaches, the site includes coaching instructions and information about local coaching clinics and how to become a coach. The site also gives information about local contact people across the country.

Do you know someone who might like to become an in-line hockey official? The site has information about officiating, as well as playing and coaching.

Perhaps you'd like to see in-line hockey players in action. You'll find many photos on this site.

In-line hockey is popular in the United States. It's popular in other countries, as well. You can find information about the international in-line hockey scene on the USA Hockey InLine Web site.

USA Roller Sports (USARS)

USA Roller Sports
4730 South Street
Lincoln, NE 68506
www.usarollersports.org

Want to learn more about a variety of roller sports? Then this is the site for you. It provides information about roller hockey, figure skating, speed skating, and fitness skating. The links on the site will take you to information about extreme roller sports, Web sites of groups close to you, and events scheduled across the country.

Glossary

adopt	to accept and begin to use something
amateur	relating to someone who takes part in something for pleasure rather than for money
catch air	to make a skating move in which both skates are off the ground at the same time
coping	metal bar across the top of a ramp that is used for grinding (see separate glossary entry)
dominant	more important, effective, or prominent than others
donation	gift or contribution, especially a sum of money, given to a charity
drop in	to enter a ramp from the top by dropping over the edge and landing on the skates
fakie 900	to spin $2\frac{1}{2}$ revolutions backward
flat spin 720	skating move in which the skater catches air (see separate glossary entry) and does a horizontal spin with two full revolutions
grind	skating move in which the skater slides across the edge of something
liability	relating to the legal responsibility to pay for damages or costs
lubricant	oil or grease used to make something smooth or slippery
patent	to gain the exclusive right, officially granted by a government to an inventor, to make or sell an invention
polyurethane	type of strong, human-made material
professional	relating to someone who takes part in something for pay rather than pleasure
reflex	an automatic response
rocket	to make a skating grab in which both legs are straight out in front and the skater reaches to grab them; similar to a pike in diving
run	one person's turn to perform
rush of adrenaline	thrill
stance	position of skates in relation to the body
stats	stands for *statistics*, numbers that tell how well a player is doing at a sport
stunt double	person whose job it is to take the place of an actor in a scene involving danger or requiring a special skill
switch 900	skating move in which the skater changes from moving forward to backward $2\frac{1}{2}$ times
vert ramp	U-shaped piece of equipment used in aggressive in-line skating

Index